St. He~~~ C0-DUN-747

Prehistoric Creatures Then and Now

IGUANODON

By K.S. Rodriguez
Illustrated by Steven James Petruccio

STECK-VAUGHN
ELEMENTARY · SECONDARY · ADULT · LIBRARY

A Harcourt Company

www.steck-vaughn.com

Special thanks to Bob Walters of Walters and Kissinger Dinosaur Art Studios for his insights into the dinosaur art trade.

Produced by By George Productions, Inc.

Photo Acknowledgments:
Pages 18, 29: Royal Tyrrell Museum of Paleontology/Alberta Community Development; Pages 23, 27: Department of Library Services, American Museum of Natural History.

Contents

Millions and Millions of Years Ago

Once upon a time a creature as big as a fire truck lived on Earth. It could run faster than an Olympic runner. It was a plant eater and used its hard beak to snap off leaves to eat. It used its spikelike thumbs to keep itself safe from enemies.

This strange reptile was called Iguanodon.

Iguanodon was more than 16 feet (5 m) tall and 25 to 30 feet (7.6 to 9 m) long.

This animal is not made up. Its story is true. But you cannot see this strange creature today. Iguanodon lived millions and millions of years ago, in the "Age of the Dinosaurs."

Time Line ———

Mesozoic
(The era of the dinosaurs)

prosauropod

Stegosaurus

Tyrannosaurus

Triassic	**Jurassic**	**Cretaceous**
245 million to 208 million years ago	208 million to 145 million years ago	145 million to 65 million years ago

Some 245 million to 65 million years ago, dinosaurs like Iguanodon ruled Earth. Dinosaurs were reptiles that lived on land and laid eggs. It was a time before TV and radio. It was a time before people even existed.

Cenozoic
(The era of mammals, including humans)

mammoth

human

Tertiary
65 million to
5 million
years ago

Quaternary
1.6 million
years ago
to today

Iguanodon was a gentle plant eater.

    Dinosaur means "terrible large lizard." But not all dinosaurs were scary, and not all dinosaurs were large. Some were as small as chickens. Others, like Iguanodon, were large, but very gentle.

More About Iguanodon

Iguanodon lived some 130 million to 110 million years ago, in a time known as the Cretaceous period. It is one of the most widely known dinosaurs. Its bones have been found everywhere except on Antarctica.

The name *Iguanodon* means "iguana tooth." It got its name from its small, ridged teeth, which are a lot like the teeth of iguanas we see today. Iguanodon used its hard beak to cut into plants. Then it used its tongue to move the food back to its teeth.

Iguanodon's teeth were perfect for chewing ferns, mosses, and trees or palmlike shrubs.

Iguanodon's teeth were like those of today's iguana.

10

Iguanodon was so big that if it were in your house, it would fill up most of your room. Its head would probably poke through the ceiling!

Scientists believe it was fast and strong, even though it was gentle. It probably could run as fast as 20 miles (32 km) per hour—faster than the fastest human today.

Iguanodon had three toes on each back foot. It also had four fingers and a thumb on each front foot—like a human's hand. Its thumbs were very different from yours, though. They had pointy spikes.

If humans had been around, Iguanodon would have towered over them.

Iguanodon was gentle, but was able to fight off attackers with its spiked thumb.

Scientists think Iguanodon used these spikes to defend itself against meat-eating dinosaurs. It might have also used them to cut leaves and stems for food.

Scientists believe that many plant eaters traveled in packs to protect themselves from meat eaters. This is probably true of Iguanodon, too, since 31 Iguanodon skeletons were once found together. Bones tell all kinds of stories like this to the scientists who study them.

Changing Views

Scientists know a lot about Iguanodon. But there are still many things they do not know.

Iguanodon was one of the first dinosaurs ever found. Over the years it has held many secrets for scientists. Even when scientists think a mystery has been "solved," they sometimes find that their ideas are all wrong.

For many years experts believed that Iguanodon had a spike on its nose, like a rhinoceros. Much later, scientists decided that the spikes were part of Iguanodon's thumbs.

Scientists also thought at first that Iguanodon walked on all fours. Then they thought it walked on two feet. Now most experts believe it ran on two feet and walked on all four. But no one knows for sure which idea is correct.

 14

Experts believe that Iguanodon ran on two feet.

Iguanodon probably walked on all fours.

Today there are no Iguanodons alive to look at. And there are no photographs of Iguanodon to see. We must find other ways of solving the mysteries of the dinosaurs. Some people are doing just that.

 16

Gone but Not Forgotten

Scientists called paleontologists are like dinosaur detectives. They look at clues left by the dinosaurs to find out how they lived. These clues are mostly from fossils.

A fossil can be a dinosaur bone. Or it can be a print of a foot. A fossil can even be a mark of a bone or body left in a rock. Paleontologists can answer many questions about a dinosaur from a fossil, like how it looked, or what it ate. But there are some questions even fossils cannot help answer.

The biggest dinosaur mystery is, why they disappeared. Sixty-five million years ago dinosaurs disappeared from Earth. They became extinct, which means they died out. Paleontologists are not sure exactly why this happened. But they do have ideas.

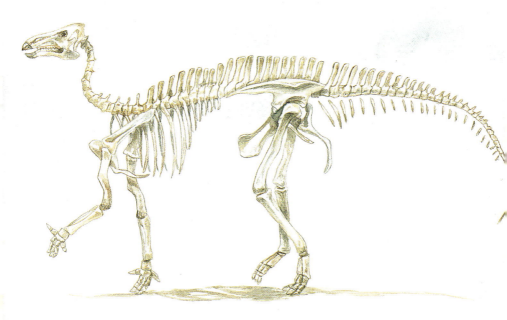

▲ An Iguanodon skeleton

◀ A dinosaur dig

One theory, or idea, is that a big rock from space, called a meteorite, crashed into Earth. When it did, it caused tidal waves and fires all over the world. Many creatures could have died right away. The crash also could have caused a giant dust cloud that blocked out the sunlight.

Without sunlight plants would have died. Without plants plant eaters like Iguanodon would have died. And without plant eaters to eat, meat eaters would have died, too.

Another theory is that the weather on Earth changed so much that the dinosaurs could not live. Some experts even think a disease killed off the creatures. Or maybe early mammals ate too many of the dinosaurs' eggs.

The Iguanodon is gone, but it is not forgotten. Paleontologists are still digging to find clues about its life.

Some experts believe that a meteorite hit Earth millions of years ago, killing off the dinosaurs.

21

The Mantells—
Husband and Wife Fossil Hunters

Dinosaur experts spend months or even years on digs for fossils. But there are fossil collectors all over the world who hunt in their own backyards. Sometimes these collectors make very important discoveries. The Mantells, an English couple who lived in the 1800s, made such a discovery.

Gideon Mantell was a doctor and scientist from England. There are many stories about how he and his wife, Mary Ann Woodhouse Mantell, discovered the Iguanodon in the early 1820s.

Iguanodon footprints

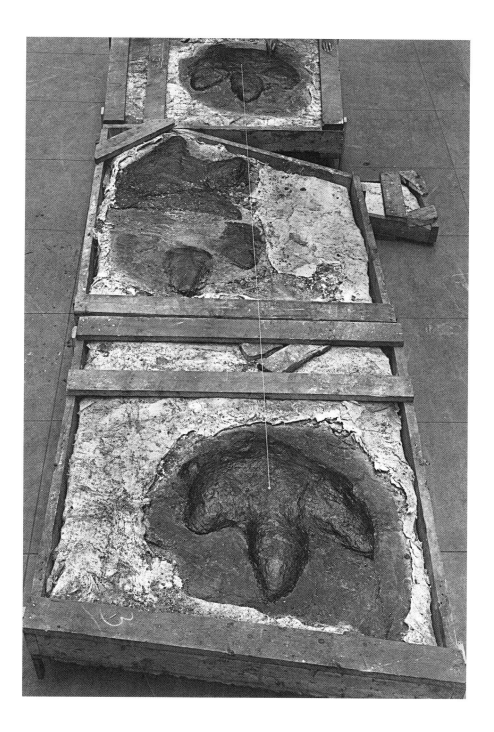

Iguanodon got close to the ground to eat plants.

One story says that Mary Ann discovered Iguanodon teeth when a road was being built by their house. Mary Ann went along with Gideon to visit a patient. When she went for a walk on the grounds, she found the fossils of the teeth.

 24

Gideon went back to the spot and found even more teeth. He gave the fossils to famous paleontologist Georges Cuvier. Cuvier declared them to be teeth from a prehistoric plant-eating reptile. At that time dinosaurs had not been discovered, or officially named yet. Gideon Mantell did more research on his own and published his study in 1825. In the study he called the creature "Iguanodon."

Drawing Dinos

If you like to draw dinosaurs, imagine doing it as a career. It is not easy. Making dinosaur pictures is hard work. After all there are no living dinosaurs or photographs for the artists to copy.

Dinosaur artists use many tools to do their work. They spend as much time researching as they do drawing or painting. First, they talk to paleontologists. Artists always work closely with these experts to get all of the details about a dinosaur right.

The artists work from the bones up. They study the bones or detailed casts of bones at museums or in private collections. Casts are impressions made of found objects. The artists

Before this mine existed, an Iguanadon walked on the muddy ground above it. Over time, that mud was covered by another layer of mud. Eventually the first layer of mud fell away, and a cast of the footprints was left on the mine ceiling.

photograph, measure, and make careful drawings of them.

Then the artists study animals that are related to the dinosaur they are drawing. They compare bones, teeth, and muscles. For example, if you were drawing an Iguanodon, you should look at the modern iguana's teeth. Sometimes the artists will even make a scale model of the creature.

Dinosaur artists research the periods in which dinosaurs lived. If more than one kind of dinosaur is in a scene, the artists must make sure the dinosaurs lived during the same time. A Tyrannosaurus rex and a Triceratops could be in the same scene. But a Tyrannosaurus rex and a Stegosaurus could not. Artists also study what Earth was like to find out which plants or other creatures may have existed at that time.

Dinosaur artists need to know as much as possible. Good dinosaur artists keep up with new discoveries. Many have special training in paleontology or take courses. Some even go on digs.

If you want to become a dinosaur artist, learn as much as you can about the prehistoric creatures. But first, learn to draw!

Young scientists enjoy finding out all they ▶ can about dinosaur fossils.

29 🦕

Glossary

Antarctica (ant-ARK-tih-kuh) Continent located around the South Pole

cast (KAST) A print of a fossil made from a mold

continent (KAHN-tuh-nunt) One of the seven major bodies of land on the earth

Cretaceous period (kreh-TAY-shus) The time period from 145 to 65 million years ago

dig (DIG) The event of digging in the earth for fossils or other dinosaur remains

dinosaurs (DIE-nuh-sores) Land-dwelling reptiles that lived from 245 to 65 million years ago

extinct (ex-TINKT) No longer existing or living

fossil (FAH-sill) Remains of ancient life, such as a dinosaur bone, a footprint, or an imprint in a rock

iguana (ee-GWAN-uh) Present-day plant-eating lizard

Iguanodon (ih-GWAN-uh-don) Large plant-eating dinosaur that lived 130 million to 110 million years ago, during the Cretaceous period

30

meteorite (MEE-tee-uh-rite) A rocky object from space that strikes Earth's surface; it can be a few inches or several miles wide

paleontologist (pay-lee-on-TAH-luh-jist) A scientist who studies fossils

prehistoric (pree-HIS-tor-ik) Referring to the time before written history

reptile (REP-tile) A group of air-breathing animals that lay eggs and usually have scaly skin

theory (THEE-uh-ree) Organized information that explains how we understand our world; an educated guess

Index